3.6
0.5pt

Mighty
MAGNETS

by Nadia Higgins

illustrations by Andrés Martínez Ricci

Content Consultant:

Paul Ohmann, PhD • Associate Professor of Physics • University of St. Thomas

visit us at www.abdopublishing.com

Published by Magic Wagon, a division of the ABDO Publishing Group, 8000 West 78th Street, Edina, Minnesota 55439. Copyright © 2009 by Abdo Consulting Group, Inc. International copyrights reserved in all countries. All rights reserved. No part of this book may be reproduced in any form without written permission from the publisher.

Looking Glass Library™ is a trademark and logo of Magic Wagon.

Printed in the United States.

Text by Nadia Higgins
Illustrations by Andrés Martínez Ricci
Edited by Jill Sherman
Interior layout and design by Nicole Brecke
Cover design by Nicole Brecke

Library of Congress Cataloging-in-Publication Data

Higgins, Nadia.
  Mighty magnets / by Nadia Higgins ; illustrated by Andrés Martínez Ricci.
     p. cm. — (Science rocks!)
  ISBN 978-1-60270-279-0
  1. Magnets—Juvenile literature. 2. Magnetic fields—Juvenile literature. I. Martínez Ricci, Andrés. II. Title.
  QC757.5.H55 2009
  538'.4—dc22
                          2008001641

Table of Contents

Where Does It Stick? 4

What Does It Work Through? . . . 10

Magnetic Fields 13

Temporary Magnets 16

Magnetic Poles 20

Mighty Magnets 28

Activity 30

Fun Facts 31

Glossary 32

On the Web 32

Index 32

Where Does It Stick?

Let's go on a mission.
A magnet-sticking mission!

Pull a magnet off the fridge
and see where it will stay.

Warning! Don't use magnets near computers or other electronics. Magnets could pull things loose and damage these devices.

4

Your magnet didn't hang on tree bark, leaves, or dog fur. These things are nonmagnetic.

It only stuck to metal things. But magnets do not stick to all metal things.

Magnets pull on iron. They also pull on metal that has a lot of iron in it, such as steel.

Paper clips, nails, and needles are made of iron. They scoot to magnets. Coins and jewelry stay put.

What Does It Work Through?

The door of your fridge doesn't look like metal. So why does your magnet stick to it? There must be iron underneath the door's colored coating.

A magnet could work through your earlobe and maybe even your fingertip. Try it!

Magnets can work through plastic, paper, and other nonmagnetic things, as long as they're thin enough.

Magnetic Fields

Tie a thread around a paper clip. Then, hold your magnet sideways. Place the tip of the paper clip to the bottom of the magnet so that it dangles. Now, gently pull the thread down. The paper clip floats!

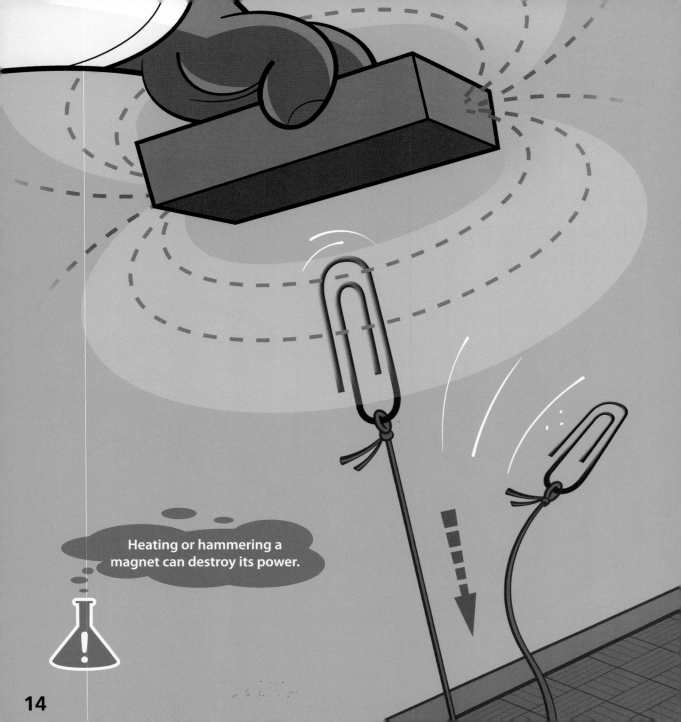

Heating or hammering a magnet can destroy its power.

14

Keep pulling and the paper clip drops to the floor.

A magnetic field is the invisible space around a magnet where its power can be felt. When the paper clip was floating, it was inside the magnetic field. When it dropped, it was outside the field.

Temporary Magnets

Hang a nail from the end of a magnet. Now touch another nail to that nail. It stays! Add more nails. How many will stay?

17

The nails turned into temporary magnets. Iron things become magnets when they are inside a magnetic field.

Test a magnet's strength. Take two magnets and see which one can hold more nails. It's not necessarily the bigger one.

But the nails won't stick to each other if the magnet is too far away. Iron things lose their power when they are outside a magnetic field.

Magnetic Poles

Rub a steel marble along a magnet. Why does the marble keep flying to the magnet's ends?

The ends are the magnet's poles. The poles are the strongest parts of a magnet.

All magnets have two poles. The poles are in different places, depending on the magnet's shape.

The poles are often marked with the letters *N* and *S*. Why?

There are two kinds of magnetic poles. *N* stands
for north pole and *S* stands for south pole.

23

Grab two magnets and try to make their north poles touch. Now try with the south poles. It's difficult.

Lay a magnet near a table's edge. Can you use another magnet to push it off the table? Don't let the magnets touch!

Poles that are alike repel, or push apart.

Now touch a south pole with a north pole. It's easy!

Poles that are different attract, or pull together.

Mighty Magnets

Now you know that magnets have power.
That power can be put to work.

The magnets inside machines could get confused by outside magnets. Keep magnets away from these devices.

Magnets are hidden inside motorized gadgets around your home. The magnets make motors go. What else do mighty magnets do?

29

Activity

Make a Compass

A compass is a tool that helps you figure out which way you're going. The needle of a compass is a magnet, and the north pole of the magnet is colored. No matter which way you turn, the colored end of the compass needle will point northward.

How can that be? A compass works because Earth itself is a giant magnet. You can make a compass needle that will always point north.

What you need:

A bar magnet, with poles marked N and S
A piece of string

What to do:

1. Tie the string around the middle of the bar magnet.
2. Ask a grown-up to tell you which way is north.
3. Hold the string and let your magnet dangle.
4. The bar magnet will slowly turn until its north pole faces north.

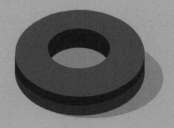

Fun Facts

Superfast maglev trains don't ride on train tracks. Powerful magnets in the train repel magnets below, and the train speeds along on a cushion of air.

The Ancient Greeks and the Chinese independently discovered the power of magnets. They realized that magnetite, a mineral found in nature, attracted iron.

Some animals, such as salmon, pigeons, and dolphins, migrate thousands of miles one way and then back again. Why don't they get lost? Scientists think their bodies have magnets that pick up Earth's magnetic field. Like compasses, the magnets guide the animals across open air and sea.

A magnet always has two poles. If you break a magnet in half, a north pole and a south pole will form in each of the two pieces. You can break a magnet into hundreds of tiny pieces and each little piece will still have two poles.

Magnets used in motors are called electromagnets. Most electromagnets are made by wrapping wire around a piece of iron. Electromagnets are temporary. When electricity flows through the wire, the electromagnet has power. When the electricity stops, it loses its magnetic field.

Special gases called plasmas are so hot, they would melt any ordinary container. The gases are held in place by a "magnetic bottle." These bottles are really just powerful magnetic fields that hold the plasma in place.

The ink used to make dollar bills has traces of iron in it. A powerful magnet could pull a dollar bill off a table.

Glossary

invisible—something that cannot be seen.

magnetic field—the area around a magnet in which its pull can attract iron.

nonmagnetic—not affected by a magnet's force.

poles—the strongest points on a magnet.

temporary magnet—a magnet that works only under certain conditions.

On the Web

To learn more about magnets, visit ABDO Publishing Company on the World Wide Web at **www.abdopublishing.com**. Web sites about magnets are featured on our Book Links page. These links are routinely monitored and updated to provide the most current information available.

Index

attract 27
body 10
coins 8
computers 4
electronics 4
fridge 4, 10
hammering 14
heat 14
iron 8, 10, 18, 19

junkyards 9
magnetic field . . . 15, 18, 19
magnetic poles . . . 21, 22, 23, 24, 25, 26, 27
motors 29
nails 8, 16, 18, 19
needles 8
nonmagnetic 6, 11
paper clip 8, 13, 15

repel 25
steel 8, 9, 20
temporary magnets . . . 18